THE STANLEY CUP PLAYOFFS

THE QUEST FOR HOCKEY'S BIGGEST PRIZE

Matt Doeden

M MILLBROOK PRESS · MINNEAPOLIS

Millbrook Press™
An imprint of Lerner Publishing Group, Inc.
241 First Avenue North
Minneapolis, MN 55401 USA

For reading levels and more information, look up this title at www.lernerbooks.com.

Main body text set in Minion Pro Regular.
Typeface provided by Adobe Systems.

Library of Congress Cataloging-in-Publication Data

The Cataloging-in-Publication Data for *The Stanley Cup Playoffs:*
  The Quest for Hockey's Biggest Prize is on file at the Library of Congress.
ISBN 978-1-5415-7838-8 (lib. bdg.)
ISBN 978-1-5415-8383-2 (eb pdf)

Manufactured in the United States of America
1-46936-47813-8/19/2019

CONTENTS

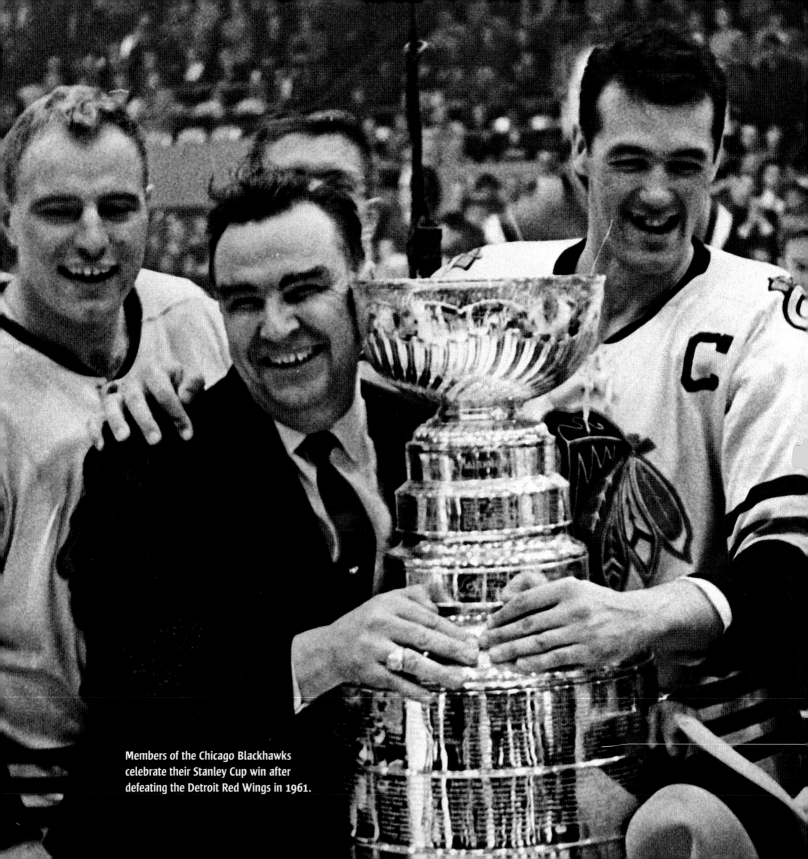

Members of the Chicago Blackhawks celebrate their Stanley Cup win after defeating the Detroit Red Wings in 1961.

INTRODUCTION

TRIUMPH ON THE ICE

The Stanley Cup playoffs are an impressive display of sights and sounds. It's the cutting of skates into a smooth sheet of ice, the ringing slap of a shot on net, the high-pitched ping as the puck bounces off the goal post. The crowd roars as players from both teams converge on the puck. The goalie's eyes shift back and forth, scanning for every possible avenue of attack. An offensive player secures the puck. He reaches back and fires. These are the playoffs, and everything rides on this shot.

In the National Hockey League (NHL), the playoffs are where legends are made. The importance of every breakaway, penalty, shot, and save is magnified. One play can be the difference between a championship and heartbreak. And every team is chasing the same prize: the Stanley Cup.

The Cup is glory and tradition. The quest to raise it in victory has triggered intense competition since the late 1800s. And passion for the game and the Cup has only grown. From just a handful of teams in the early days to more than 30 today, the NHL has prospered and made the Stanley Cup one of the greatest prizes in sports.

LORD STANLEY'S CUP:
A HISTORY OF HOCKEY'S BIGGEST PRIZE

The sun beat down on the Nevada desert on May 30, 2018, sending outdoor temperatures soaring to nearly 100°F (38°C). It wasn't the weather that would make people think about hockey. Yet the world's most popular winter sport was exactly what sports fans in Las Vegas—and around the world—were thinking about.

The heat outside may have been sweltering. But inside Las Vegas's T-Mobile Arena, a sheet of glimmering white ice was the center of attention. That's because the Vegas Golden Knights were hosting the Washington Capitals in Game 2 of the Stanley Cup Finals—the championship of the NHL.

The NHL has always lagged in popularity behind other major team sports, such as football, baseball, and basketball. But in 2018, Las Vegas had given the NHL a boost in national interest. The Golden Knights simply weren't supposed to be there. They were an expansion team playing its first season as a franchise. It was a squad built of young stars and castoffs from other NHL teams. This was the sort of underdog story that could captivate sports fans who otherwise may have paid

The Washington Capitals pose with the Stanley Cup
after winning the NHL championship in 2018.

After stunning the hockey world by winning their division during the regular season, the Golden Knights had torn through the Western Conference playoffs with a 12–3 record. Then they electrified their fan base by beating the Capitals in Game 1 of the Finals, 6–4. It seemed a real possibility that Vegas could hoist the Stanley Cup in their first season.

The Capitals, however, had other plans. The team had existed since 1974 and had exactly as many Stanley Cup titles as Vegas—none. They were led by Alexander Ovechkin, a goal-scoring sensation who was looking to cement his place as NHL royalty by leading his team to a title.

Game 2 marked a turning point in the series. Early in the second period, Ovechkin buried the puck in the back of the Vegas goal to give Washington a lead they would not surrender. Goaltender Braden Holtby turned back the final 15 shots to snuff out an attempted Vegas comeback, and the Capitals evened the series with a 3–2 victory. Washington went on to win each of the next three games to claim the Cup and dash Vegas's hopes of a storybook ending.

In the end, it wasn't a nail-biting Finals. Washington was clearly the superior team, and after losing the first game, they had little trouble taking firm control of the series. The Golden Knights were denied the Cup, but the franchise's opening chapter had been unlike any NHL team—or major sports team—had ever seen. It served as a reminder to sports fans everywhere that the hard-hitting, always surprising Stanley Cup playoffs rarely went according to form and that any team, any year, can rise up to challenge for the most famous trophy in sports.

THE CUP IS BORN

No trophy in professional sports is more steeped in tradition than the NHL's championship trophy, Lord Stanley's Cup. In 1889 Canada's governor general, Sir Frederick Arthur Stanley, Lord Stanley of Preston, attended the Winter Carnival in

Montreal, Quebec. While there he saw his first hockey game between the Montreal Hockey Club (Montreal HC) and the Montreal Victorias. Stanley was captivated by the game, which was exploding in popularity in Canada. He became an avid hockey fan and so did his sons, Arthur and Algernon, who started a team of their own.

Lord Stanley was born in London, England, in 1841.

At the time, hockey was a loosely organized sport featuring mainly local leagues and amateur players. But Arthur and Algernon were drawn to the idea of crowning a single champion. They urged their father to create a trophy that would be awarded to the best team. Stanley liked the idea. In 1892 he bought a silver, bowl-shaped trophy from London silversmith G. R. Collis and Company and declared that it would stand as a symbol for the champions of Canadian hockey. It cost about $50. Stanley had the words "Dominion Hockey Challenge Cup" engraved on one side of the trophy. On the other were the words "From Stanley of Preston."

A year later, Stanley and his trustees, a group of people who made decisions on the rules for the Cup, awarded the trophy to Montreal HC, the champions of the Amateur Hockey Association of Canada (AHAC). The trustees believed that the AHAC was the top league in Canada. At the time, hockey leagues didn't have playoff systems. The championship went to the team with the best regular-season record. However, in 1894, four AHAC teams tied for first place with 5–3–0 records. League officials decided on a playoff series to determine the one true champion. It was the very first Stanley Cup playoffs.

A four-team playoff should have been a tidy affair. However, Quebec—one of the four teams—declined to take part. That left the Ottawa Generals and two teams from Montreal to vie for the Cup. Since the games would be held in Montreal, the

Montreal HC were the AHAC champs for many years prior to their Stanley Cup win. Billy Barlow is seated at the far right.

league gave Ottawa a first-round bye. On March 17, 1894, Montreal HC and the Montreal Victorias played the first Stanley Cup playoff game. On the strength of two goals by forward Billy Barlow, Montreal HC won the hard-hitting contest 3–2, earning the right to face Ottawa in the Final. In that game, Barlow scored twice again, and Montreal HC defended its title with a 3–1 victory over Ottawa.

THE CHALLENGE CUP ERA

The decision to give the Stanley Cup to the AHAC champion had come with more than its share of controversy. Other hockey leagues protested and demanded the right to play for the Cup. The trustees agreed and allowed one team from each league to challenge for the Cup once per year.

The decision marked the beginning of the Challenge Cup era in hockey. It was a wild, free wheeling time during which the rules about who was the champion were ever-shifting and often nonsensical. The first challenge came in 1895 from Queen's University in Kingston, Ontario. The divide between college hockey and club hockey had not yet been made, so college teams were able to lay claim to the Cup.

Queen's challenged Montreal HC, the 1894 champions. However, the Montreal Victorias had already won the 1895 AHAC championship, which meant that Queen's was challenging a team that did not currently hold the title. The trustees made a decision that might seem bizarre in any era. Queen's would win the Cup if it won the game. If Montreal HC won the game, then the Montreal Victorias would remain the champions. It was a contest for the highest honor in hockey, and the AHAC champion Victorias didn't even play in it!

In the end, the Queen's team was no match for the bigger, faster AHAC team. Montreal HC won easily 5–1, winning the Cup for their crosstown rivals.

The Challenge Cup era really kicked into gear in 1896 when the Winnipeg Victorias of the Manitoba Hockey League challenged—and beat—the reigning AHAC champs, the Montreal Victorias. The team's name, *Victorias*, which honored the queen of England, was common at the time. It was the first Stanley Cup match that featured an eastern team and a western team, and it marked the beginning of a rivalry between the two regions of Canada. Suddenly, the AHAC was not at the top of the hockey world, and the Cup passed back and forth from team to team—and from coast to coast.

Challenges were fast and furious. In 1908 the Montreal Wanderers were forced to defend the Cup five times. Meanwhile, top teams began to lure the best players by paying them large sums of money. Over time, the mostly amateur sport evolved into a professional one. Teams that didn't pay their players—or didn't pay much—simply could no longer compete for the Cup. In 1908 the Allen Cup was introduced as a

The Montreal Victorias *(pictured)* won the Stanley Cup in 1895 when Montreal HC beat Queen's University in a challenge match.

trophy for amateur-only teams, and the Stanley Cup became strictly a professional hockey trophy.

In 1914 the trustees decided that teams should have to defend the Cup only once a year at the end of their league's season. The wild and chaotic challenge system was abandoned, and a playoff system between various league champions was adopted. The format changed from year to year, but the era of the Challenge Cup was over.

THE UNDERDOG THISTLES

During the Challenge Cup era, championship teams were generally from Canada's largest cities. But in 1907, the Thistles, a team from the small Ontario mining and lumber town of Kenora, got their chance to challenge for the Stanley Cup. Kenora was home to between 4,000 and 5,000 people—tiny compared to Montreal, Ottawa, Winnipeg, and other cities whose teams had hoisted the Cup.

Known first as the Rat Portage Thistles, the team first formed in 1894 as a junior team of boys aged eleven to fourteen. Among them were Tommy Phillips, Tom Hooper, Billy McGimsie, and Si Griffis—all of whom went on to the Hockey Hall of Fame. As the team's young core grew, they moved up to play in the senior division.

Challenges from small-town teams weren't a new thing, but it rarely went well for the challengers. In 1905 the Dawson City Yukoners made the trip east to challenge the Ottawa Silver Seven in a scheduled five-game series. But after losing the first two games by a combined score of 32–4, the Yukoners had seen enough. They packed their things and headed home.

Any Montreal fans expecting a similar result from the Thistles were quickly disappointed. The series between the Thistles and the Montreal

The Thistles showed that a small-town team could be great. Tommy Phillips, the hero of Game 1, is in the center.

Wanderers was set for two games with aggregate scoring, meaning the scores would be added together to determine the winner. The smaller Thistles attacked with speed. Tommy Phillips was the star of the first game, scoring four times and handing Montreal a shocking 4–2 defeat. In Game 2, Montreal countered by trying to press their physical advantage. They tried to manhandle the younger, faster team, but all they accomplished was racking up 55 penalty minutes. The Thistles kept up their attack, winning 8–6 to claim the Cup.

The Thistles' reign didn't last long. Just two months later, the Montreal Wanderers challenged them to a rematch and won handily. The Thistles disbanded less than a year later. But their legacy as one of the great underdogs in Stanley Cup history lives on.

THE ROAD TO THE NHL

The NHL has its origins in the National Hockey Association (NHA). The NHA was a league of eastern Canadian teams in cities such as Montreal and Toronto. The league's first game was in 1910 between the Cobalt Silver Kings and the Montreal Canadiens. But by 1917, disputes between owners caused the National Hockey Association to suspend operations. Some of the owners formed a new league to take its place: the NHL. At first, the NHL was merely a replacement league for the National Hockey Association, but it faced some challenges. For instance, no team was in Toronto, one of Canada's largest cities, and only three teams played the

The 1924-1925 Victoria Cougars included eleven players and head coach Lester Patrick *(bottom row, center)*. Modern NHL teams have twenty-three players.

first season. But over the next decade, the NHL, led by stars such as Joe Malone and Howie Morenz, dominated hockey. NHL teams generally offered the richest contracts to players, and a talent gap opened between the NHL and the other hockey leagues. In 1925 the Victoria Cougars of the Western Hockey League (WHL) became the last non-NHL team to win the Cup. The Cougars—and the WHL—dissolved a year later.

The Prairie Hockey League stepped in to fill the role left by the WHL. But that league was doomed. The NHL purchased many of the WHL's player contracts and used them to expand and further take control of professional hockey in North America. When the Prairie Hockey League folded, the NHL was the only major professional hockey league left. The Stanley Cup became the official championship trophy of the NHL in 1947.

THE LEAGUE TRANSFORMS

During the 1920s and 1930s, the NHL's size changed from year to year. By 1926 the league had ten teams, and it was dominated by defense. The rules of the game made scoring exceedingly difficult, and at least partially as a result, the game lagged in popularity outside of Canada. In the 1928–1929 season, Montreal Canadiens goalie George Hainsworth recorded 22 shutouts in just 44 games. The lack of goal scoring was becoming a major problem, and the NHL scrambled to fix it.

In 1929 the league made a major rule change. For the first time, forward passes inside an offensive zone were allowed. The rule served to set free the offensive game, and goal scoring more than doubled. Offense increased so dramatically that a year later the league introduced the modern offside rule to slow down offenses, requiring that the puck enter the offensive zone before any offensive player does. The league continued to tweak other rules as the decades passed. More and more, hockey started to resemble the game fans know today.

Johnny Gottselig *(bottom)* played for the Black Hawks from 1928 to 1945, winning the Stanley Cup in 1934 and 1938.

Events in the United States and around the world also altered the NHL. In the 1930s, the Great Depression, a severe economic decline that lasted from 1929 to about 1939, forced some NHL teams out of business. Then World War II (1939–1945) followed. Many players enlisted or were drafted, and NHL leaders believed that able-bodied men should serve their countries rather than play hockey. In fact, the NHL stated that "it was opposed to employment by any club of any person who should properly be in active service for his country." Hockey's player pool was depleted, leaving those deemed unable or too young for military service to make up NHL rosters. In 1943 the Brooklyn Americans folded, leaving just six NHL teams: the Boston Bruins, Chicago Black Hawks, Detroit Red Wings, Montreal Canadiens,

New York Rangers, and Toronto Maple Leafs. For two-and-a-half decades, these Original Six teams composed the entire league. While other major team sports, such as baseball and football, were expanding, professional hockey remained a small and often overlooked affair.

By the 1960s, the professional sports scene had changed dramatically. Baseball, football, and basketball were more popular than ever, and expansion continued for these pro leagues. Hockey grew as well. In 1967 the NHL was ready to grow with six new expansion franchises. The league doubled in size after adding the California Seals, Los Angeles Kings, Minnesota North Stars, Philadelphia Flyers, Pittsburgh Penguins, and St. Louis Blues. The twelve NHL teams were split into the Eastern and Western Conferences. The expansion rush was on. By 1974 the league had grown to 18 teams. As the league grew, its playoff format evolved, with twelve teams taking part in the playoffs beginning in 1974. That number swelled to 16 in 1979, its modern-day total.

The Minnesota North Stars (*pictured*) played their first game on October 21, 1967, against the California Seals.

UNKNOWN ORIGINS

No one is sure exactly when or where ice hockey got its start. Similar stick-and-ball games were popular in the British Isles dating back to at least the 1700s. Some evidence suggests that the game began there. Others believe that the game we know today originated in Canada during the early 1800s. Some trace the game to King's College School in Ontario, Canada. Boys at this college would gather on frozen ponds to compete in a game they called ice hurley, a name and game that may have evolved into ice hockey.

WINTER PASTIME.

Ice hockey may have started as an outdoor game on frozen ponds and rivers.

Regardless of who invented the game, most experts agree that the first indoor ice hockey game was held in Montreal in 1875. However, even this game, which featured nine players on each side, probably bore little resemblance to the sport we know today. Players used a flat piece of wood as a puck instead of a ball, which could go into the stands and injure spectators.

The first formal team, the McGill University Hockey Club, formed in 1877. More teams soon followed as the ice hockey craze swept through Canada. Over the decades, the rules changed, and the game slowly evolved into the one modern fans know and love.

The origin of hockey remains a hotly debated issue. Canada lays claim to its creation, though recent research points more and more to Europe being the sport's birthplace. Regardless, one thing is certain. The game grew and developed in Canada, and it remains Canada's national sport.

2 THRILLERS, COMEBACKS, AND UPSETS:

THE GREATEST GAMES OF THE STANLEY CUP PLAYOFFS

More than a century of Stanley Cup action has given fans an abundance of thrills, chills, and heartache. From the greatest upsets and comebacks in NHL history to its most nail-biting overtime thrillers, NHL stars have provided plenty of excitement on the ice. Read on to learn about some of the greatest games in Stanley Cup playoff history.

THE LONGEST GAME

DETROIT RED WINGS 1, MONTREAL MAROONS 0
GAME 1, STANLEY CUP SEMIFINALS, MARCH 24, 1936

Defense was on display when the Red Wings and Maroons squared off in Game 1 of the 1936 Stanley Cup semifinals. A *lot* of defense. The teams skated for more than 170 minutes without scoring a single goal!

It wasn't pretty hockey. As the overtime sessions piled up, the condition of the ice grew worse and worse. By the fifth overtime, players were mounting wild—sometimes reckless—charges just in hopes of ending the game. Detroit's Herbie Lewis almost won it by firing a shot past Montreal goalie Lorne Chabot. But the shot was just wide. It clanged off the post, and play continued.

Finally, late in the sixth overtime period, relief came from an unlikely source. Rarely used Detroit rookie Moderre "Mud" Bruneteau had scored only two goals all season. But with three and a half minutes remaining in the sixth extra session, he intercepted a pass and blasted a shot past Montreal's Chabot, ending the longest game in NHL history. Gleeful Detroit fans began throwing money onto the ice to show their gratitude—cash that Bruneteau happily scooped up.

Bruneteau got the glory for ending the game, but the true hero was probably Detroit goalie Normie Smith. Smith, who lost 12 pounds in the grueling marathon, stopped all 92 shots he saw, an NHL record that still stands. Detroit went on to win the series and then beat the Toronto Maple Leafs to claim the Stanley Cup.

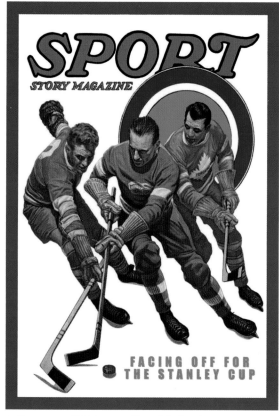

In the 1930s, NHL fans could read fictional hockey stories in magazines.

DOWN BUT NOT OUT

TORONTO MAPLE LEAFS 3, DETROIT RED WINGS 1
GAME 7, STANLEY CUP FINALS, APRIL 18, 1942

The 1942 Stanley Cup Finals were not going well for the Toronto Maple Leafs. The Detroit Red Wings had come out firing in the first three games of the series, building up a 3–0 advantage in the best-of-seven series. Toronto had been the better team throughout the season, but in the Finals, it was Detroit taking what appeared to be a stranglehold on the series. Toronto was on life support after blowing a two-goal lead in Game 3, and Detroit fans were eager to watch their squad hoist the Stanley Cup.

FROM THE WHA TO THE MODERN NHL

Bobby Hull won the WHA Most Valuable Player award in 1973 and 1975 with Jets.

The NHL was growing, but some people believed the pace was too slow. In 1972 the World Hockey Association (WHA) formed to compete with the NHL. The WHA placed teams in major US cities and in midsize Canadian cities that did not yet have an NHL team. League owners in the WHA lured top talent with lucrative contracts, sparking a bidding war between the leagues. The WHA made its biggest splash when superstar Bobby Hull left the NHL to sign a ten-year, $2.75 million contract with the Winnipeg Jets. At the time, it was an unimaginable salary for a hockey player, and it immediately gave the new league the credibility it needed to compete with the established NHL. A year later, the WHA signed the biggest star in hockey at the time: Gordie Howe.

The WHA set forth on an aggressive plan to expand. But many experts now believe that the young league stretched itself too thin. By the 1976–1977 season, its finances were drying up. The big contracts that had lured many former NHL players were gone, and much of the league's talent migrated back to the NHL. There were exceptions—most notably a young core of players on the Edmonton Oilers led by Wayne Gretzky and Mark Messier. But even as the Oilers were on the rise, the writing was on the wall for the WHA. The league could not survive. By June of 1979, only six WHA franchises remained. The league negotiated with the NHL, which agreed to take on four of the surviving teams—including the up-and-coming Oilers. The merger marked a new era of professional hockey, and Gretzky became its face.

Gretzky readies his stick in a game during his rookie season with the Edmonton Oilers.

Throughout the decades, professional hockey had featured many superstars, from Maurice "Rocket" Richard to Gordie Howe. But the league never had anyone like Wayne Gretzky. The Great One combined skill, grace, and a unique ability to see the game. Gretzky rewrote the NHL record books, leading his Oilers to four Stanley Cup titles before the team shockingly traded him to the Los Angeles Kings in 1988. Gretzky's star power attracted fans by the millions and helped the league reach levels of popularity never before seen.

With the rise of internationally born players in the 1990s and 2000s, the NHL was once again tapping new markets, signing television deals, and packing arenas. And the league's feature attraction remained the Stanley Cup playoffs. For fans, nothing could compare to the intensity—and the finality—of rival teams clashing on the ice in pursuit of the Stanley Cup.

With the series headed to Detroit, a Red Wings' victory seemed in the bag. According to an April 11 Associated Press news story, "Detroit's third straight victory in the best-of-seven series for the trophy emblematic of world hockey supremacy was so convincing that it became almost a certainty, even in the Toronto camp, that the series will not be carried from Detroit ice where the Wings are unbeaten in 13 successive games."

Desperate for a spark, Toronto head coach Clarence "Hap" Day benched star players Gordie Drillon and Bucko McDonald for Game 4. The Maple Leafs responded with a hard-fought 4–3 victory that ended with an all-out brawl on the ice.

It may not have been clear at the time, but the tide had turned. Toronto scored early and often in Game 5, blowing out the Red Wings 9–3. Once again, the game was marred by fighting and cheap shots, with the violence spilling into the stands as fans joined in the bad behavior.

Game 6 started out as a defensive struggle. After a scoreless first period, Toronto's Don Metz stole the puck deep in the Detroit zone and snuck a backhanded shot past goaltender Johnny Mowers. That was enough for Toronto goalie Turk Broda, who stopped every shot that came his way. Toronto won the game 3–0, and stunned Detroit fans were left wondering how a series that had seemed nearly over after three games was suddenly headed to a deciding Game 7—in Toronto.

Ted Kennedy led the Toronto Maple Leafs to five Stanley Cups between 1943 and 1957. He played with the team for his entire 14-year career.

More than 16,000 fans flocked to the final game. They were treated to some of the best hockey of the series. Detroit took a 1–0 lead in the second period. The Red Wings, desperate to fend off yet another collapse, tried to lock down on defense. They held the lead into the third period. That's when Toronto launched an extreme assault on the Detroit goal. The Maple Leafs outshot the Red Wings 16–7 in the period, scoring three times. The arena erupted as the final horn sounded. The Maple Leafs had done the unthinkable. They were the first—and still the only—team ever to overcome a 3–0 series deficit in the Stanley Cup Finals.

"We did it the hard way," said Toronto coach "Hap" Day. "I had my doubts right up until that final bell rang."

THE ROCKET SEALS IT

MONTREAL CANADIENS 3, BOSTON BRUINS 1
GAME 7, STANLEY CUP SEMIFINALS, APRIL 8, 1952

Professional hockey in 1952 was very different from the modern game. Players didn't wear helmets, and serious injuries, such as concussions, were often ignored—especially in Game 7 of the Stanley Cup semifinals.

That was the situation facing the Montreal Canadiens in the second period of their winner-take-all series finale against the Boston Bruins. During a dash up the ice, Rocket Richard—one of the biggest stars of the day—controlled the puck and rushed toward the goal. As Richard made a move, he failed to spot Boston defenseman Hal Laycoe. Laycoe lowered a shoulder toward the unsuspecting Richard, who took a stick to the face in the collision. Richard's head slammed into the knee of a teammate on his way down.

The superstar lay bleeding and unconscious on the ice as a silent crowd looked on. In the modern game, such an injury would send a player to the hospital for tests. The idea of returning to the game would be unthinkable. But this was a different era. Montreal's team doctor, Gordon Young, waved away a stretcher as Richard regained consciousness.

Richard's teammates helped him back to the bench, where Dr. Young stitched up the gash on his face. Richard lost consciousness a second time while he was being stitched. Young advised Richard not to return to the game, and Richard sat out until there were about four minutes remaining. Then he returned to the ice.

The score was tied 1–1, and Montreal's Emile Bouchard sent a pass ahead to Richard. As a Boston defender went for a poke check, trying to knock the puck loose, Richard zipped it ahead and then charged forward to recover the puck. Richard pushed off another defender who was closing in and then drove hard to the net. He faked a shot, fooling goalie Jim Henry. Henry moved to the left, and Richard pounced, firing a shot into the opposite corner of the net.

Rocket Richard won eight Stanley Cups with the Canadiens.

"My legs were alright, but I was dizzy," Richard said. "I heard the crowd yell, and by that time I was too dizzy to see."

It was all the Canadiens needed. They added an empty-net goal at the end, securing a trip to the Finals. They lost to the Red Wings, but Richard's amazing goal remains one of the most iconic in NHL history. Even so, Richard had lost consciousness twice and risked additional serious harm during those last four minutes. Fortunately, the modern game relies on helmets and rules about when players may return to the ice after concussions to limit such hazardous finishes.

TRAGEDY AND CHANGE

On January 13, 1968, the Minnesota North Stars hosted the California Seals in a regular-season game. At the time, players were not required to wear helmets. During the first period, Minnesota center Bill Masterton carried the puck toward the California zone. A defender converged on Masterton, hitting him with a hard but legal check. The collision knocked Masterton backward. He landed head-first on the ice. The crowd at the Met Center grew silent as he lay there, unmoving, with blood coming from his nose and mouth.

Masterton was carried off the ice and rushed to a hospital. Two days later, Masterton died from what doctors called massive brain injuries. He remains the only NHL player to die as the direct result of an injury suffered during a game.

Masterton's death sparked debate in the hockey world. Until that point, few players wore helmets. Some players looked down on those who did. Yet Masterton's death—which may have come in part because of previous head injuries he'd suffered in his career—was enough to spark change. More and more players began wearing helmets, although their use remained voluntary for another decade. It wasn't until 1979 that the NHL passed a rule requiring helmets for new players while allowing veterans who entered the league before the rule change to continue without them. The last player to play without a helmet was Craig MacTavish in 1997.

Craig MacTavish gets ready for action with the Edmonton Oilers in 1987.

THE MIRACLE ON MANCHESTER

LOS ANGELES KINGS 6, EDMONTON OILERS 5
GAME 3, WESTERN CONFERENCE FIRST ROUND, APRIL 10, 1982

With a star-studded lineup led by Wayne Gretzky, the Edmonton Oilers seemingly could do no wrong in the 1980s. But even one of hockey's greatest dynasties was capable of slipping up from time to time. And that was never truer than in Game 3 of their first-round playoff series with the Los Angeles Kings.

It was a series that wasn't supposed to take long. The Oilers were the NHL's best team, and they'd finished a stunning 48 points better than the Kings during the regular season. Even when Los Angeles pulled off a Game 1 upset, few imagined that the Oilers were in much trouble. Edmonton bounced back to win Game 2 and appeared firmly in control when they stormed out to a big lead in Game 3.

Fans packed into the Great Western Forum on Manchester Boulevard in the Los Angeles suburb of Inglewood, and they watched in stunned silence as the Oilers employed their relentless attacking style. Even an Edmonton penalty wasn't enough to give Los Angeles life. Late in the first period, the Kings were on a power play. But Gretzky got the puck, neatly skated through the Kings' defense, and drove home an electric shorthanded goal.

The Oilers didn't let up in the second period, extending the lead to 5–0. It was a rout, and the confident young Oilers weren't shy about letting the Kings know who was in charge. According to Kings defenseman Jay Wells, "Not only were they mocking us, but the coach was, too. . . . That put a fire in our tail."

By the start of the third period, the Oilers appeared to be on cruise control. The Kings, meanwhile, were annoyed by the arrogance and disrespect they felt the young Oilers were showing them. Jay Wells scored early in the third period to put Los Angeles on the board, and they quickly followed that up with a power-play goal from Doug Smith.

Steve Bozek (*right*) of the Kings fights for the puck. He would score the tying goal later in the game.

The comeback bid stalled. Ten minutes passed with no scoring, and Edmonton's 5–2 lead looked more than safe. Then, with about six minutes remaining in the game, the Kings stole the puck. Forward Dean Hopkins zipped a pass to Charlie Simmer, who tried to jam the puck into the corner of the net as he was falling down. Edmonton goalie Grant Fuhr was in position to block the shot. But at that moment, Edmonton defenseman Randy Gregg, rushing in to clear the puck, accidentally ran into his own goalie. Gregg knocked Fuhr back, and Simmer's shot reached the goal. It was 5–3.

Soon after, with each team skating four men to a side because of penalties, Los Angeles struck again. Kings forward Steve Bozek charged toward the net and then left a drop pass for Mark Hardy. Hardy reared back and unleashed a shot that sailed past Fuhr. Suddenly it was 5–4, and the Forum crowd was roaring.

Still down by one goal, the Kings pulled their goalie with a minute to play. Los Angeles was on a power play, which meant they were skating with a two-player advantage. That allowed them to control the puck, but the scrambling Oilers managed to shut down one opportunity after the next.

The crowd grew louder—and more anxious—as time was slipping

In 1982 Gretzky led the NHL with an astounding 212 points, but he couldn't save the Oilers from a Game 3 collapse.

away. With less than 10 seconds to go, Hardy took a shot, but Fuhr deflected it. The puck trickled back out in front of the net. Kings' left winger Steve Bozek anticipated the rebound and came crashing toward the net. Bozek collected the puck and whisked a backhanded shot before Fuhr had time to react. Goal! The Kings had tied it with just five seconds remaining in regulation. It was on to overtime.

The Kings' comeback almost came to a swift end in overtime. Goalie Mario Lessard left the net to gain possession of a stray puck, but he collided with one of his own defensemen. Edmonton's Mark Messier collected the puck with an open net in front of him. Hardy hustled back to throw himself between Messier and the net, and Messier's backhanded attempt missed to the right of the goal. Lessard scrambled back between the pipes, and the overtime session went on.

Soon after, the teams prepared for a face-off in the Edmonton end. Doug Smith won the puck for Los Angeles, sending it backward toward center ice. Rookie Daryl Evans attacked, drawing his stick back for a hard blast. His shot caught Fuhr unprepared. The puck zoomed past Fuhr's glove and into the back of the net. The celebration erupted in the stands and on the ice, where the Kings mobbed Evans. They had come back from a 5–0 deficit to win. The game, nicknamed the Miracle on Manchester, remains the greatest comeback in NHL playoff history. Los Angeles would go on to eliminate the powerful Oilers in Game 5, coming back from a score of 2–0.

THE EASTER EPIC

NEW YORK ISLANDERS 3, WASHINGTON CAPITALS 2
GAME 7, DIVISION SEMIFINALS, APRIL 18, 1987

The fans who filed into Capital Centre in Landover, Maryland, for Game 7 of the division semifinals expected a good game. After all, the teams had proven to be evenly matched, splitting the first six games of the series, and there was no reason to believe the finale would be anything but a nail-biter. But even with high expectations, no one was prepared for what followed. The game, which started on a Saturday evening, stretched long into the night, spilling into the early hours of Easter Sunday, earning it the nickname the Easter Epic.

Washington controlled the play early but didn't find the net until Mike Gartner scored in the closing minute of the first period. Each team scored once in the second period, and the Capitals carried a 2–1 lead into the third. The officials seemed determined to call as few penalties as possible, leading to a very rough and hard-hitting game. That suited the Capitals, who worked to outmuscle the Islanders as they tried to protect their slim lead.

With about five minutes remaining, New York was on the attack. Center Bryan Trottier tried to sneak a backhanded shot past Capitals goalie Bob Mason. Mason had been almost unbeatable in net all night, and he saw the shot coming. But as he moved to make the stop, his right skate broke. Suddenly, his momentum stopped, and his ankle was left with no support. Trottier's shot bounced off one of Mason's pads and deflected into the goal. Tie game! Mason's backup, Pete Peeters, hadn't seen action all game. So rather than switch goalies, the Capitals left Mason in net— with one good skate. Luckily for

Pat LaFontaine slaps the game-winning shot in the fourth overtime of Game 7.

Washington, the final five minutes of regulation passed without any scoring.

Mason returned to the ice for overtime with his skate fixed. The play was fast and furious, but both Mason and New York goalie Kelly Hrudey turned away every shot they faced. Twenty minutes passed without any scoring. Double overtime was no different. New York's Robert Woods came close to scoring, but his shot clanged off a post. After 100 minutes of hockey, the game remained knotted at two goals apiece.

By the third overtime, the pace of the game had slowed. Players on both sides were exhausted. The Islanders looked a bit fresher and controlled the action, but Mason didn't let any of New York's scoring chances get by him. The final seconds of the period ticked away, and the game entered a fourth overtime session, something that hadn't been seen in an NHL game since 1951.

More than 120 minutes of hockey had left both teams spent, but the Islanders appeared to have just a bit more energy in the fourth overtime. Eight minutes into the period, New York's Ken Leiter brought the puck into the Washington zone. Leiter zipped a pass out in front of the goal. Gord Dineen took the pass and skated around the back of the net, hoping to stuff it in. But Washington's defense was there to snuff out his attack, forcing him to take a difficult shot that Mason blocked. The puck bounced right to the stick of New York's star center, Pat LaFontaine, who wasted no time collecting the puck, spinning, and rifling a hard shot on net. With several players gathered in front of the goal, Mason never saw the shot coming. The puck dinged off the left post and bounced into the net. The exhausted Islanders swarmed onto the ice in celebration. After 128 minutes of hard-fought hockey, the game was finally over.

"I don't think I've ever shot a puck the same way since," said LaFontaine. "I just spun around because the puck came to me at an interesting angle, and I just wanted to

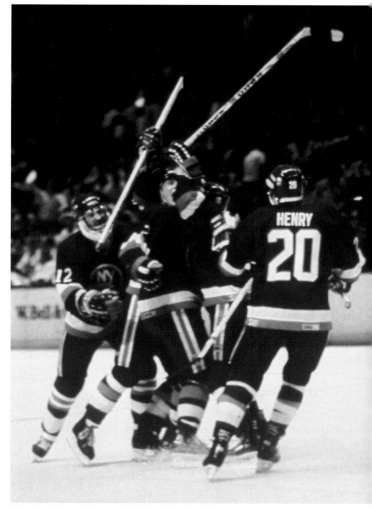

The Islanders celebrate their hard-fought victory. Including time-outs and other stoppages, the game lasted more than six hours.

shoot it and hope for the best, because everything Kelly Hrudey and Bob Mason saw, they stopped. I remember the puck being off on its side, so I didn't catch it flat and it kind of knuckled. I heard the post and thought, 'Oh,' as if it didn't go in, but then I saw Mason drop to his knees and I saw our guys start to drop, and then it was just unbelievable emotion for about a minute. Then we just all collapsed."

THE WAITING IS OVER

NEW YORK RANGERS 3, VANCOUVER CANUCKS 2
GAME 7, STANLEY CUP FINALS, JUNE 14, 1994

New York Rangers fans thought their team was cursed. The team won the Stanley Cup in 1940. More than half a century passed before they would do so again. It was a string of near misses. They'd made the Finals in 1950, 1972, and 1979 but lost all three times.

The Rangers show off the Stanley Cup in style in 1940.

OTHER HOCKEY CHAMPIONSHIPS

The Stanley Cup is the pinnacle of men's professional hockey. But it's not the only major hockey championship in the world. Read on to learn about some others.

THE OLYMPICS

Every four years, both men and women compete for the biggest prize in international hockey, an Olympic gold medal. Men's ice hockey has been part of the Olympics since 1920. Women's ice hockey was added in 1998. Canada's eight gold medals lead the way for the men, while the three golds of the United States are the most in the women's tournament.

Monique Lamoureux-Morando of the US women's national team skates against Finland in the 2018 Winter Olympic Games.

ICE HOCKEY WORLD CHAMPIONSHIPS

Aside from the Olympics, the Ice Hockey World Championships is the biggest international men's hockey tournament in the world. The annual tournament is split into divisions, with the top nations competing in the Division I bracket. The tournament is open to both amateur and professional players. As of 2018, team Russia (formerly the Soviet Union, a group of 15 republics) has won the most gold medals with 27. Canada is a close second with 26.

IIHF WOMEN'S WORLD CHAMPIONSHIPS

The Women's World Championships, held by the International Ice Hockey Federation, has been held annually or semi-annually since 1991. Canada and the United States have dominated the field. Those two teams have met in every gold-medal match since the tournament began. Canada has won gold ten times, while the United States has won eight.

NCAA MEN'S ICE HOCKEY CHAMPIONSHIP

Since 1971, the top men's college hockey team in the United States has been crowned at the NCAA Men's Ice Hockey Championship. The final four teams, called the Frozen Four, face off in a single-elimination bracket to determine the winner. The University of Michigan leads the field with nine national championships.

The University of Minnesota Duluth Bulldogs pose with their trophy after winning the 2019 NCAA Frozen Four Men's Hockey National Championship.

NCAA WOMEN'S ICE HOCKEY TOURNAMENT

The top collegiate women's teams face off each year in the NCAA Women's Ice Hockey Tournament. The single-elimination tournament began in 2001. The University of Minnesota's six national titles are the most all time, while the University of Minnesota Duluth is second with five championships.

THE ISOBEL CUP

The National Women's Hockey League is a professional women's hockey league that started in 2015. Each year, the top teams compete for the league's trophy, the Isobel Cup. The cup is named for Lady Isobel Gathorne-Hardy, the daughter of Lord Stanley. The Boston Pride won the first Isobel Cup in 2016. Other champions include the Buffalo Beauts in 2017, the Metropolitan Riveters in 2018, and the Minnesota Whitecaps in 2019.

In 1994 the Rangers seemed destined to end the curse. Superstar center Mark Messier led the Rangers to the league's best record and then famously guaranteed a win in Game 7 of the Eastern Conference Finals. Messier delivered on his promise, and the Rangers were four wins away from ending the curse.

In the Stanley Cup Finals, they were poised to finish off the Vancouver Canucks quickly. The Rangers built a 3–1 series lead, only to watch the Canucks win Game 5 and Game 6 to force a deciding final game. Ranger fans were understandably uneasy as they filed into Madison Square Garden for Game 7. Would this be just another crushing disappointment in a long series of failures? Fans may have been nervous, but the Rangers were a veteran team and not easily unnerved by Vancouver's comeback.

What followed was one of the most thrilling 60 minutes of hockey the Stanley Cup playoffs had ever provided. The New York crowd was electric as the Rangers built a 2–0 lead. Early in the second period, the Rangers were on a power play, looking to extend that lead. But a long pass found Vancouver's Trevor Linden all alone, streaking toward the New York goal. Linden didn't let the breakaway go to waste and tapped in a backhanded score to cut the lead to one.

Craig MacTavish of the Rangers holds the Stanley Cup after New York defeated the Vancouver Canucks four games to three in 1994.

New York answered later in the period. After a mad scramble in front of the Vancouver goal, the puck trickled out to Messier along the left post. Messier took the shot, banging the puck off the goaltender's leg and into the goal. The New York fans roared, and the Rangers were back in control, 3–1.

Once again, Vancouver was on the brink of defeat. Early in the third period Linden scored again—this time on a power play to make the score 3–2. As the third period clock ticked away, the action grew fast and furious. Vancouver launched wave after wave of attacks on the New York goal, but the goaltender denied every shot. With five minutes remaining, the Canucks nearly tied the game on a shot by Nathan LaFayette that dinged off the post. Vancouver never eased up on the pressure, but the Rangers were there to snuff out every charge. As the final horn sounded and ticker tape rained down on the victorious Rangers, Messier leaped into the air, and then wept as he accepted the Stanley Cup.

"The waiting is over!" shouted Rangers play-by-play announcer Sam Rosen. "The New York Rangers are the Stanley Cup champions! And this one will last a lifetime!"

KANE'S OVERTIME WINNER

CHICAGO BLACKHAWKS 4, PHILADELPHIA FLYERS 3
GAME 6, STANLEY CUP FINALS, JUNE 9, 2010

The winning goal in this game was one of the most exciting in NHL history—yet almost no one saw it. The Chicago Blackhawks were in the midst of a Stanley Cup drought that spanned half a century since they last won in 1961. But with a 3–2 series lead in the Finals over the Philadelphia Flyers, the Blackhawks were in position to end the wait.

The Flyers, meanwhile, were the surprise team in the playoffs. The seven seed had torn through the Eastern Conference bracket with a series of upsets, and the

The Chicago Blackhawks celebrate Patrick Kane's second-period goal during Game 6 of the 2010 Stanley Cup Finals.

Philadelphia fans were eager for just one more.

Chicago took a 3–2 lead into the third period. For a time, it looked like Chicago goalie Antti Niemi would make that lead hold up as he stopped shot after shot. But with less than four minutes remaining in the game, Philadelphia winger Ville Leino gained control of the puck in his own end. Leino pushed the puck up the ice, weaving through Chicago defenders. He streaked toward the right post and then centered the puck toward a swarm of skaters in front of the net. The puck bounced off the stick of a Blackhawk and then off the leg of Philadelphia winger Scott Hartnell. In goal, Niemi was unable to track the bouncing puck as it trickled inside the left post. Tie game!

It was a stroke of good luck for the Flyers, but their luck did not hold in overtime. Four minutes into the extra period, the Blackhawks were on the attack. Patrick Kane controlled the puck along the left side. He carried it wide of the goal before flicking a casual shot on net. Kane's shot came from a nearly impossible angle—almost parallel to the goal—and he was likely looking to create a rebound rather than score. The Philadelphia goalie hugged the left post as he moved to deflect the puck.

The puck suddenly was loose in front of the goal, and Philadelphia fans cheered as the Flyers began a charge in the other direction. But seconds later a whistle blew. Chicago's bench emptied onto the ice in celebration. The referees had ruled that Kane's shot had crossed the goal line, ending the sudden-death overtime—and the series. Philadelphia players and fans looked on in disbelief. No horn had sounded. No one had actually seen the puck go in. But an official review confirmed the call. Kane's shot really had gone into the net—even if almost no one in the building had seen it. The goal was good, and the Blackhawks celebrated their first Stanley Cup since 1961.

FLYING HIGH

PHILADELPHIA FLYERS 4, BOSTON BRUINS 3
GAME 7, EASTERN CONFERENCE SEMIFINALS, MAY 14, 2010

The Boston Bruins weren't supposed to lose the Eastern Conference Semifinals to the Philadelphia Flyers. Boston dominated the first three games of the series to take a commanding 3–0 series lead. But the Flyers fought back, winning the next three games to tie it up.

Game 7 featured more of what happened in the first three games. Boston dominated early, scoring three times within the first 15 minutes to take control. The Boston crowd roared in support, waving thousands of yellow towels as they watched their team overwhelm the Flyers. Philadelphia's hopes of completing the comeback appeared dim at best. Only two teams had ever come back from a three-goal deficit in a Game 7.

After the third Boston goal, Philadelphia head coach Peter Laviolette called his team's only time-out of the game. Traditionally, coaches save the time-out for late-game situations, but Laviolette felt the game, and the series, slipping away. He told his team that they needed just one goal before the end of the period to get back in the game. And the Flyers delivered. With three minutes left in the first period, forward James van Riemsdyk delivered an ugly shot that broke his stick. The puck deflected off a Boston defender and then slipped under the pads of Boston goalie Tuukka Rask.

With that much-needed shot of confidence, the comeback was on. The once-deafening Boston crowd grew nervously quiet in the second period when Scott Hartnell scored to pull the Flyers to within a goal of the Bruins. Just minutes later, Philadelphia's Danny Briere carried the puck behind the Boston net, curled around to the far post, and stuffed it in. And just like that the game was tied. Philadelphia had overcome a 3–0 deficit to tie the series, and now they'd overcome a 3–0 deficit to tie the score in Game 7. All that remained to be seen was whether they could finish the job.

James van Riemsdyk *(center)* controls the puck amid a group of Boston defenders.

The opening half of the third period was a defensive battle, but with just under nine minutes remaining, Boston made a critical error. During what should have been a routine shift change, the Bruins were penalized for having too many men on the ice. The result was a two-minute power play for the Flyers.

With time running out on the power play, the Flyers remained patient. They zipped the puck around the Boston zone as the four Boston skaters

Simon Gagne's goal secures the Stanley Cup for the Flyers.

gave chase. The puck came to Mike Richards to the right of the goal. Richards unleashed a hard slap shot. Goalie Tuukka Rask made the stop, but the rebound went straight to the stick of Flyer winger Simon Gagne. Gagne followed with a lightning-fast shot into the far upper corner of the net.

Boston did everything it could to tie the game in the last nine minutes, but Flyers goalie Michael Leighton turned away every attempt. The clock hit 0:00, and the Bruins could only watch as Philadelphia celebrated one of the most remarkable comebacks in NHL history.

3 MEMORABLE MOMENTS:

FROM THE PHANTOM FOG TO THE PHANTOM GOAL

ometimes it's a single play or performance that stays with hockey fans. It's a scoring explosion, a freak play, a blown call, or something out of the ordinary that have them talking for days, weeks, and even years. Read on to learn more about some of the most memorable moments in Stanley Cup playoff history.

SUIT UP, COACH

NEW YORK RANGERS 2, MONTREAL MAROONS 1
GAME 2, STANLEY CUP FINALS, APRIL 5, 1928

In 1928 NHL teams generally didn't have backup goalies. That put the New York Rangers in a difficult spot in Game 2 of the Stanley Cup Finals when goalie Lorne Chabot was forced to leave the game with an injury.

Ranger coach Lester Patrick was scrambling, but he came up with a plan. Ottawa Senators goalie Alex Connell was in the crowd watching the game. Lester asked the Rangers' opponent, the Montreal Maroons, for permission to use Connell.

Lester Patrick suited up as a goalie for this 1940 photo.

Not surprisingly, the Maroons declined the request. That left the Rangers with few options. It was a time when NHL rosters were small, and the team couldn't spare a skater. So Patrick did the only thing he could think to do. He strapped on the goalie pads himself.

Patrick was a former player, but he'd never been a goalie. The Rangers focused on playing hard-hitting defense, trying to minimize the number of shots their coach would have to see. And it worked! Patrick allowed only one goal during his time in the net, and the Rangers won the game 2–1 in overtime.

A SCARE FOR HOWE

TORONTO MAPLE LEAFS 5, DETROIT RED WINGS 0
GAME 1, STANLEY CUP SEMIFINALS,
MARCH 28, 1950

In 1950 Gordie Howe was the talk of the NHL. The up-and-coming superstar scored 35 goals during the regular season, which was second most in the league. More importantly, he led the Detroit Red Wings to the top overall seed in the Stanley Cup Playoffs.

Gordie Howe (left) stares down Teeder Kennedy (right) in a game from the 1950s.

The Red Wings squared off with the Toronto Maple Leafs in the first round. They were fierce rivals. The first game of their series was hard-hitting and dominated by the Maple Leafs. It would have been a forgettable contest if not for one play that almost ended the career—and the life—of one of hockey's legendary players.

In the third period, leading 4–0, Toronto's Teeder Kennedy controlled the puck. Howe charged at Kennedy, intent on jarring the puck free. He lowered his shoulder to lay a hard hit. But Howe mistimed his charge. He lost his balance and hit Kennedy with a glancing blow. Kennedy powered forward, sending the helmetless Howe flying face first into the boards with a sickening thud.

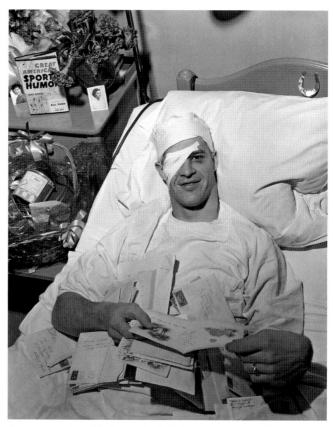

Howe poses with gifts he received during recovery from his head injury.

Kennedy immediately knew Howe was in trouble. "I saw Howe lying on the ice with his face covered with blood," he said. "I couldn't help thinking what a great player he was and how I hoped he wasn't badly hurt."

But Howe *was* badly hurt. His skull was fractured, and he was clinging to life. Howe was carried off the ice and rushed to a hospital. The swelling in his brain was causing deadly pressure in his head. It was a race to save his life. Doctors had to drill a hole through his skull to relieve the pressure. Howe later recovered, but the young star was told that he'd never play hockey again.

Howe had other plans though. Six months later, he was back on the ice to open the 1950–1951 season. He played in all 70 of Detroit's games and led the league with 86 points. That was 20 more than second-place Maurice Richard. The legend of Gordie Howe was just beginning. But it nearly ended before it ever began.

It was also a happy ending for the Red Wings after Game 1 in 1950. They came back without Howe to beat the Maple Leafs and then the New York Rangers to claim the Stanley Cup.

ORR'S FLYING GOAL

BOSTON BRUINS 4, ST. LOUIS BLUES 3
GAME 4, STANLEY CUP FINALS, MAY 10, 1970

NHL history is filled with iconic moments. But few can match the one that NHL defenseman Bobby Orr gave Boston Bruins fans in 1970.

Boston hadn't won the Stanley Cup in 29 years—an amazing drought considering that the NHL had been a six-team league through most of that time. Boston fans were hungry for a championship. So when the Bruins took a 3–0 series lead over the St. Louis Blues in the 1970 Stanley Cup Finals, they were ready to celebrate.

The Blues hadn't been competitive in the first three games, but their play improved with the series at stake in Game 4. St. Louis held a 3–2 lead deep into the third period. But with less than seven minutes to play, Boston winger Johnny Bucyk scored to tie the game. The rest of the third period was scoreless, sending the game to sudden-death overtime.

Just 40 seconds into the overtime period, Boston had the puck in the St. Louis zone. Orr was near the boards to the right of the goal. He slid a pass to teammate Derek Sanderson and then darted toward the net. Sanderson completed the give-and-go play by passing it right back to the streaking Orr in front of the goal. Orr slapped

Bobby Orr *(center)* soars above the ice in one of the NHL's most famous photographs.

it in just as a defender tripped him. A photographer captured an iconic image of Orr sailing through the air as the puck went into the net. Orr's flying goal ended Boston's long Cup drought, and the party in Boston was on. Even after all of these years, Orr's game-winner remains one of the most celebrated goals in NHL history.

THE PHANTOM FOG

BUFFALO SABRES 5, PHILADELPHIA FLYERS 4
GAME 3, STANLEY CUP FINALS, MAY 20, 1975

Game 3 of the 1975 Stanley Cup Finals was one of the strangest games in NHL history. The Philadelphia Flyers traveled to take on the Buffalo Sabres in Buffalo Memorial Auditorium. It was a hot and humid day, and the auditorium didn't have air conditioning. As the ice cooled the warm, humid air, a blanket of fog formed over the ice, leaving the game to be played in a haze.

The strangeness was just beginning because the fog wasn't the only thing in the air. In the first period, a bat swooped back and forth over the ice. As the period dragged on, the bat flew lower and lower, seemingly unconcerned with the action. At one point during a game stoppage, players gathered at a face-off circle and watched the animal flying just a few feet above them.

The fog, however, became the bigger issue as it continued to grow thicker. It blanketed the ice, seeming to swallow up the players' skates and lower legs. It grew so thick that fans in the stands couldn't even tell what was happening on the ice. The players looked like shadows, and the puck was shrouded from view. Auditorium workers tried to fan away the fog but were unsuccessful.

The game went on despite the fog. The teams were deadlocked at 4–4, forcing an overtime session

Flyers goalie Bernie Parent tries to keep his eyes on the puck through the thick fog. Temperatures near the ice were close to 90°F (32°C) that day.

that saw the fog grow even thicker. Play was stopped over and over as rink workers desperately tried to clear the air. Then after 19 minutes, Buffalo's Rene Robert finally ended the game with a goal. Afterward, Robert admitted that he wasn't even trying to score when he shot the puck. He just hoped to create a rebound for one of his teammates. But with the thick fog, Philadelphia goalie Bernie Parent couldn't track the puck and it slipped past him.

"I saw Robert's shot too late for me to come out and stop it," said Parent. "I'm surprised the overtime took so long. It was hard to see the puck from the red line. If three men came down and one made a good pass from the red line, you couldn't see the puck. A good shot from the red line could have won it."

Buffalo may have won the game, but the Flyers went on to win the series. Some fans think that the Sabres—who have never won a Stanley Cup—suffer from the curse of the phantom fog.

FIGHTING IN HOCKEY: THE BRAWL THAT CHANGED THE GAME

PHILADELPHIA FLYERS 4, MONTREAL CANADIENS 3

GAME 6, CONFERENCE FINALS, MAY 14, 1987

For good or bad, fighting has long been a part of hockey. Some hockey experts and fans argue that fighting is good for the game. It allows players to police their own behavior. Others believe it's a black eye on the sport. Rule changes in recent decades have greatly decreased the number of fights in hockey, but critics say that there are still too many and that the fights send the wrong message to young fans.

The sport's history is littered with brawls, but few were more memorable than the one that broke out between the Montreal Canadiens and Philadelphia Flyers in 1987. Most of the time, a hockey fight happens after a big hit or a cheap shot. But this fight took place before the game even started.

Both teams had gone through warm-ups and were skating off the ice. Montreal forward Claude Lemieux often liked to end warm-ups by shooting a puck into the opposing team's empty net. For some reason, this got under the skin of Philadelphia's Ed Hospodar. "Don't do it,

John Kordic (*right*) was involved in two fights during the pregame brawl.

Claude," Hospodar warned as Lemieux prepared to shoot.

For a moment, it seemed Lemieux would honor the request. He began skating off without taking his customary shot. But as the Flyers left the ice, Lemieux backtracked. He took the shot just as he always had.

Hospodar was not pleased. He charged Lemieux, and the fight was on. Players from both sides streamed onto the ice—some of them not even fully suited up. In total, 36 players joined in. The only two who didn't were each side's starting goalie. The brawl dragged on for almost ten minutes before it finally broke up.

The game ended with a 4–3 victory for the Flyers. But the headline was the fight. The NHL, which had long tolerated such behavior, had seen enough. The playoff brawl sparked a new wave of anti-fighting rules that drastically reduced such large-scale fights. In the modern game, fights still take place. But the age of the bench-clearing brawl is all but gone, mostly as a result of this fight.

Lemieux *(second from left)* fights for the puck during the Conference Finals.

A BLOWN CALL AND THE DAWN OF A DYNASTY

NEW YORK ISLANDERS 5, PHILADELPHIA FLYERS 4
GAME 6, STANLEY CUP FINALS, MAY 24, 1980

Few games in NHL history are more steeped in controversy than Game 6 of the 1980 Stanley Cup Finals. It's a game that New York Islander fans remember as the start of one of the league's great dynasties. Meanwhile, fans of the Philadelphia Flyers remember it for one bad call that may have cost their team a shot at the Stanley Cup.

Denis Potvin, New York Islanders captain, raises the Stanley Cup.

The Islanders led the series 3–2 and were looking to finish off the Flyers in Philadelphia. The key play came in the first period with the score tied 1–1. The Islanders controlled the puck and were breaking toward the Philadelphia zone. Clark Gillies carried the puck into the zone along the left side and dropped a pass back to teammate Butch Goring. Goring then zipped a pass across the ice to the streaking Duane Sutter, who rifled a slap shot. Philadelphia goaltender Pete Peeters couldn't react in time, and the Islanders were in front.

Only it wasn't as simple as that. Gillies was well inside the Philadelphia zone when he left his pass for Goring. By rule, no offensive player can beat the puck into the zone. The play was a clear offside, and should have been whistled dead. Somehow, the referees missed the obvious call, much to the distress of Flyers coaches, players, and fans.

The game went to overtime, tied 4–4. About seven minutes into the extra period, New York's John Tonelli darted toward the Philadelphia goal. As the defense collapsed toward him, Tonelli slid a pass to Bobby Nystrom. All alone, Nystrom tucked a shot into the bottom left corner of the goal.

The celebration was on for the Islanders. It was the team's first Stanley Cup title and the beginning of a streak of four consecutive championships. Philadelphia fans went home disappointed and disgusted, feeling like a bad call had robbed them of their chance to force Game 7.

GRETZKY DOMINATES

EDMONTON OILERS 10, CALGARY FLAMES 2
GAME 3, DIVISION SEMIFINALS, APRIL 17, 1983

Wayne Gretzky was nicknamed The Great One for a reason. Gretzky could do it all. His uncanny ability to see exactly how plays would unfold always left him a step ahead of the competition. So it's no surprise that he put together some of the greatest individual playoff performances in history. One of his best came in 1983. Gretzky's Oilers were battling their fierce rivals, the Calgary Flames, in the division semifinals.

Gretzky wasted little time asserting himself. In the first period, the Flames were on a power play, but Gretzky intercepted a pass at center ice. He slid the puck over to teammate Paul Coffey and then streaked toward the goal. Coffey passed it back, and Gretzky did the rest, sliding it under the pads of the diving goalie. Less than a minute later Gretzky scored again on a breakaway.

Gretzky skates for the Oilers during a home game in the 1980s.

Gretzky and the Oilers kept adding to the lead. Gretzky scored two more goals in the second period. And he added three assists, giving him a seven-point night. The Flames never had a chance. Edmonton won the game 10–2 and went on to eliminate the Flames in five games.

HULL'S PHANTOM GOAL

DALLAS STARS 2, BUFFALO SABRES 1

GAME 6, STANLEY CUP FINALS, JUNE 19, 1999

Some Buffalo fans talk about the curse of the phantom fog—a reference to the strange fog game held in Buffalo during the 1975 Stanley Cup Finals (see pp. 44–45).

Brett Hull (top) and Jason Woolly slide into the goal.

So perhaps it's fitting that the Sabres lost in their only other Finals appearance on what many have termed a phantom goal.

Although the phantom goal remains a source of controversy, it was only part of one of the longest games in NHL history. The game was held in Buffalo with Dallas leading the series 3–2. Dallas was one win away from its first Stanley Cup title, while Buffalo was desperate to stay alive in the series.

The series had been dominated by defense and goaltending with the teams combining for just 19 goals through the first five games. The legendary Dominik Hasek was in goal for Buffalo, while Ed Belfour stood between the pipes for Dallas. Both men were up to the task in a low-scoring Game 6.

Dallas opened the scoring in the first period. Winger Jere Lehtinen took a pass from Mike Modano near the left face-off circle. Despite having a defender draped all over him, Lehtinen slipped the puck just inside the goalpost to put the Stars in front.

Buffalo, which had struggled to generate offense all series, answered in the second period. Center Stu Barnes got the puck near the right circle. He uncorked a hard shot that caught Belfour leaning the wrong way. Buffalo fans erupted as their team celebrated its first goal in nearly two full games.

From that moment, the game was all about defense. Hasek and Belfour matched each other save for save. Tied 1–1, the game stretched into overtime where the hard-nosed, defensive struggle continued. No one scored in the 20-minute overtime session, sending the game to double overtime.

Just under five minutes remained in the second overtime when the game finally ended. Dallas controlled the puck in the Buffalo zone. Modano fired a shot on goal that Hasek blocked. The rebound trickled out in front of the goal, where Brett Hull was lurking. Hasek, lying down on the ice, scrambled in a desperate attempt to get between Hull and the goal, but Hull was too quick, slipping the puck in before Hasek could recover.

As Hull *(bottom center)* shoots, his left skate is clearly in the goal's painted area.

But replay showed that Hull's skate was in the crease, the painted area in front of the goal. Many players and fans believed that Hull's goal had been illegal. Confusion reigned among Buffalo fans as officials reviewed the call. Buffalo's bench was convinced that the call would be reversed. But the officials confirmed that the goal was good, and the game was over. Dallas had won.

Outcry from fans, players, and coaches was immediate. The NHL insisted that according to a recent rule change, the call was correct, saying that Hull had gained possession of the puck when he was outside of the crease. Dejected Buffalo fans disagreed. Boos rained down on the arena as Dallas celebrated. In protest, the Sabres players refused to leave the locker room. And the debate among fans and media reached a fever pitch.

"It makes me very mad," Hasek said after the game. "I still cannot believe it. I don't understand what the video judge is doing. Maybe he was in the bathroom. Maybe he was sleeping. Maybe he doesn't know the rule."

Even twenty years later, hockey experts still disagree about whether Hull's goal should have counted. But it did, giving Dallas its first Stanley Cup in one of the NHL's most exciting, and controversial, Finals games in history.

CROSBY'S UNBELIEVABLE GOAL

PITTSBURG PENGUINS 7, PHILADELPHIA FLYERS 0
GAME 1, DIVISIONAL SEMIFINALS, APRIL 11, 2018

Game 3 of the opening-round series between the Penguins and Flyers would have been a largely forgettable affair if not for one jaw-dropping moment. It came from one of the game's biggest superstars, forward Sidney Crosby, in the second period.

Already leading 4–0, the Penguins were on a rush into Philadelphia territory. Pittsburgh's Jake Guentzel blazed deep into the zone, curling around the back of the Flyers' net. As the Philadelphia defense rushed toward him, Guentzel slid a pass out

Crosby swats the puck out of midair and into the goal.

to a wide open Brian Dumoulin. Dumoulin quickly shot the puck, but it deflected off a defender's stick. The puck fluttered and spun into the air.

Crosby, standing just beyond the left post, saw the puck coming. The superstar lifted his stick and batted at the chest-high puck, tapping it backhanded past goalie Brian Elliot. It was just one goal in a 7–0 Pittsburgh rout. But it was a goal that nobody would ever forget, and it served as a reminder of why Crosby is one of the best in the game.

THE FUTURE OF THE STANLEY CUP PLAYOFFS:

IMPROVED SAFETY AND A WORLDWIDE LEAGUE

The Stanley Cup playoffs are bigger than ever. With worldwide television coverage, packed arenas, and hard-hitting rivalries, it doesn't get any better for hockey fans. The game has changed a lot since Lord Stanley created a trophy for the greatest hockey team in the land. And those changes continue, from rules to protect players to a move toward globalization. What does the future hold for the NHL's greatest spectacle? What might the game look like in the coming decades?

THE DANGERS OF CTE

The NHL has come a long way in improving player safety since the early 1900s. Back then, players didn't wear helmets. Goalies had no protection for their faces, and many paid the price. Hockey is, by its nature, a violent game, but modern rules and protective gear give players the best possible protection.

Yet safety concerns remain a real issue for the league. In recent years, players have become more aware of chronic traumatic encephalopathy (CTE), a degenerative brain disease caused by repeated trauma to the head. CTE contributes to changes in mood and behavior and the ability to control impulses, and it can lead to depression and loss of cognitive and memory function. In 2018 more than 300 former players sued the league, arguing that the NHL failed to do enough to protect them from CTE. Although NHL officials claimed in court that no proof existed to tie CTE to hockey, they agreed to a cash settlement with the players.

Regardless of the NHL's legal stance in court, the league will have little choice but to confront

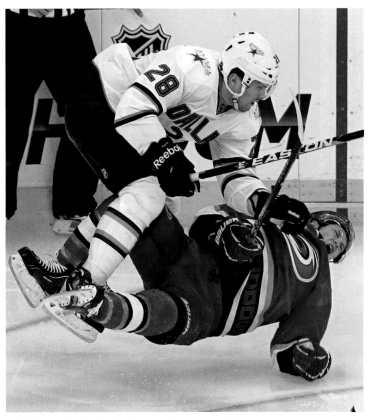

Jeff Skinner *(bottom)* missed games in three straight seasons due to concussions.

the issue of traumatic brain injuries. In the coming decades, the league and players may need to take more drastic measures to protect players. Technology may improve helmets and other safety gear, but the league may have to change rules that have been part of the game for a century.

During all those years, few plays have excited fans more than a hard check. Will those days be over? Will the NHL ban body checks? And if the league does, how will fans react to a major change in the sport they love? There are no easy answers, but the issue of CTE isn't going away any time soon.

EXPANSION AND GLOBALIZATION

The NHL started as a strictly Canadian league. It quickly expanded to the United States, where it slowly made its way south to warmer and warmer climates. Until 1961 the league featured just six teams. Since then, the NHL has exploded in popularity and in size. With the addition of the Vegas Golden Knights in 2017, the league currently features 31 teams spread across the United States and Canada.

For the first half century of its existence, the NHL was made up of players from Canada and the United States. That began to change in 1965 when Sweden's Ulf Sterner joined the Boston Bruins. Sterner played only four games in the league, but he marked the beginning of a slow but steady influx of European talent to North America. The success of European stars such as Jari Kurri and Esa Tikkanen helped establish what became known as the European Invasion. By 1990, about four percent of NHL players were European born, and by 2010, that figure had swelled to roughly 30 percent. It should be no surprise then that as more and more European-born players entered the league, the NHL's popularity in Europe grew.

In recent years, the league has made moves to capitalize on the global interest. In 2007 the Anaheim Ducks and Los Angeles Kings traveled to London, England, for a pair of regular-season NHL games— the first ever played in Europe. In 2010 NHL teams traveled to take on top European clubs in a series

The Vegas Golden Knights and the Washington Capitals battle during the 2018 Stanley Cup Finals.

of exhibition games. Then in 2017, the league started its Global Series, which has seen regular-season games played in Sweden, Finland, Germany, and other European countries. Meanwhile, the NHL has begun to schedule more afternoon games, which are friendlier to European television audiences.

Teams in Sweden and Finland, featured in this game from 2019, are no strangers to intense hockey action.

According to many experts, an NHL expansion into Europe is inevitable. According to NHL deputy commissioner Bill Daly, the league has investigated the idea of placing an entire division of teams in Europe.

"I think it would be a real positive statement to create the first really trans-ocean league," said Donald Fehr, executive director of the NHL Players Association in 2018. "I think it would be an extraordinary achievement for everybody. Hopefully [it will happen] sooner or later."

There will be many obstacles to clear before a European division could become a reality. Europe generally lacks NHL-style arenas. Travel and scheduling could be problematic, and the league would have to address any security concerns players might have about playing overseas. But none of these challenges seem too difficult to overcome, and it's not hard to imagine that one day a team from London, Berlin, or Helsinki could hoist the Stanley Cup, making it a truly international trophy.

STANLEY CUP CHAMPIONS (NHL ERA)

1927	Ottawa Senators	1959	Montreal Canadiens	1991	Pittsburgh Penguins
1928	New York Rangers	1960	Montreal Canadiens	1992	Pittsburgh Penguins
1929	Boston Bruins	1961	Chicago Black Hawks	1993	Montreal Canadiens
1930	Montreal Canadiens	1962	Toronto Maple Leafs	1994	New York Rangers
1931	Montreal Canadiens	1963	Toronto Maple Leafs	1995	New Jersey Devils
1932	Toronto Maple Leafs	1964	Toronto Maple Leafs	1996	Colorado Avalanche
1933	New York Rangers	1965	Montreal Canadiens	1997	Detroit Red Wings
1934	Chicago Black Hawks	1966	Montreal Canadiens	1998	Detroit Red Wings
1935	Montreal Maroons	1967	Toronto Maple Leafs	1999	Dallas Stars
1936	Detroit Red Wings	1968	Montreal Canadiens	2000	New Jersey Devils
1937	Detroit Red Wings	1969	Montreal Canadiens	2001	Colorado Avalanche
1938	Chicago Black Hawks	1970	Boston Bruins	2002	Detroit Red Wings
1939	Boston Bruins	1971	Montreal Canadiens	2003	New Jersey Devils
1940	New York Rangers	1972	Boston Bruins	2004	Tampa Bay Lightning
1941	Boston Bruins	1973	Montreal Canadiens	2005	NONE (Season canceled due to labor dispute)
1942	Toronto Maple	1974	Philadelphia Flyers		
1943	Detroit Red Wings	1975	Philadelphia Flyers		
1944	Montreal Canadiens	1976	Montreal Canadiens	2006	Carolina Hurricanes
1945	Toronto Maple Leafs	1977	Montreal Canadiens	2007	Anaheim Ducks
1946	Montreal Canadiens	1978	Montreal Canadiens	2008	Detroit Red Wings
1947	Toronto Maple Leafs	1979	Montreal Canadiens	2009	Pittsburgh Penguins
1948	Toronto Maple Leafs	1980	New York Islanders	2010	Chicago Blackhawks
1949	Toronto Maple Leafs	1981	New York Islanders	2011	Boston Bruins
1950	Detroit Red Wings	1982	New York Islanders	2012	Los Angeles Kings
1951	Toronto Maple Leafs	1983	New York Islanders	2013	Chicago Blackhawks
1952	Detroit Red Wings	1984	Edmonton Oilers	2014	Los Angeles Kings
1953	Montreal Canadiens	1985	Edmonton Oilers	2015	Chicago Blackhawks
1954	Detroit Red Wings	1986	Montreal Canadiens	2016	Pittsburgh Penguins
1955	Detroit Red Wings	1987	Edmonton Oilers	2017	Pittsburgh Penguins
1956	Montreal Canadiens	1988	Edmonton Oilers	2018	Washington Capitals
1957	Montreal Canadiens	1989	Calgary Flames	2019	St. Louis Blues
1958	Montreal Canadiens	1990	Edmonton Oilers		

SOURCE NOTES

10 https://web.archive.org/web/20070930080711/http://www.legendsofhockey.net:8080/LegendsOfHockey/jsp/
   SilverwareTrophyWinner.jsp?tro=STC&year=1893-94

11 https://www.sportsnet.ca/hockey/nhl/kenora-thistles-owned-stanley-cup/

15 https://thehockeynews.com/news/article/rules-that-changed-the-game

19 https://thehockeywriters.com/the-wha-a-look-back-40-years-later/

13 https://www.habseyesontheprize.com/2007/01/kenora-thistles-1907-stanley-cup.html
   https://www.sportsnet.ca/hockey/nhl/kenora-thistles-owned-stanley-cup/

18 https://thehockeywriters.com/who-invented-hockey/
   http://www.birthplaceofhockey.com/origin/overview/
   https://thehockeynews.com/news/article/do-you-think-hockey-was-invented-in-canada-think-again

19 https://books.google.com/books?id=Qm6CDwAAQBAJ&pg=PA49-IA2&lpg=PA49-IA2&dq=#v=onepage&q&f=false

20 https://www.nhl.com/news/this-date-in-nhl-history-march-24/c-279805016

23 https://www.si.com/nhl/2016/06/09/1942-stanley-cup-final-comeback-toronto-maple-leafs-detroit-red-wings-recap

24 https://www.si.com/nhl/2016/06/09/1942-stanley-cup-final-comeback-toronto-maple-leafs-detroit-red-wings-recap

25 Kevin van Steendelaar, "Recalling The Rocket's Greatest Goal," SB Nation, April 8, 2012.
   https://www.habseyesontheprize.com/2012/4/8/2932519/recalling-the-rockets-greatest-goal

25 Ibid.

27 Ryan Kennedy, "ORAL HISTORY: THE MIRACLE ON MANCHESTER, 35 YEARS LATER," The Hockey News, May18,
   2017. https://thehockeynews.com/news/article/oral-history-the-miracle-on-manchester-35-years-later

30 https://thehockeynews.com/news/article/recalling-the-easter-epic-25-years-on

32 Adam Proteau, "Recalling the Easter Epic 25 Years On," The Hockey News, August 2, 2012. https://thehockeynews.com/
   news/article/recalling-the-easter-epic-25-years-on

36 https://www.youtube.com/watch?v=8gxj0ZWMmuk

37 Jim Cerney, "Stanley Cup Finals Flashback: June 14, 1994," NHL.com, June 13, 2009. https://www.nhl.com/rangers/
   news/stanley-cup-finals-flashback-june-14-1994/c-493982

39 https://www.nytimes.com/2010/05/15/sports/hockey/15flyers.html
   https://www.youtube.com/watch?v=WbAwzDNpmtA

39 https://www.nhl.com/news/flyers-complete-comeback-rally-for-game-7-victory/c-529231

35 https://www.ncaa.com/news/icehockey-men/article/2018-10-10/most-ncaa-mens-hockey-championships

44 "Toronto Maple Leafs vs Detroit Red Wings: The Night Teeder Kennedy Almost Killed Gordie Howe,"
   GreatestHockeyLegends.com, March 28, 2013. http://www.greatesthockeylegends.com/2012/12/toronto-maple-leafsvs-
   detroit-red.html

45 https://www.youtube.com/watch?v=nkvrc9y9MRo
   https://www.history.com/this-day-in-history/bobby-orr-leads-bruins-to-stanley-cup-title
   http://bobbyorr.net/goal/goal.php

47 Jeff Z. Klein, "Neither Player Nor Bat Was Ready for the Fog," New York Times, June 6, 2014. https://www.nytimes.
   com/2014/06/07/sports/hockey/the-sabres-and-flyers-played-a-low-visibility-game-in-1975.html

54 https://thehockeynews.com/news/article/most-memorable-moment-of-brett-hulls-career-still-tainted-for-some

54 "Stars Win Stanley Cup In 3 OTs," CBS News, June 20, 1999. https://www.cbsnews.com/news/stars-win-stanley-cup-in-
   3-ots/

54 https://www.youtube.com/watch?v=oR3yaf1PbBs&feature=onebox

57 https://www.usatoday.com/story/sports/nhl/2018/11/12/tentative-settlement-reached-in-nhl-
   concussionlawsuit/38484627/

57 https://www.wsj.com/articles/no-headline-available-1392050064

58 https://thehockeywriters.com/the-evolution-of-europeans-in-the-nhl/

58 https://www.bardown.com/fascinating-nhl-nationality-breakdown-shows-the-growth-of-hockey-around-the-worldover-
   the-years-1.894809

59 David Shoalts, "NHL Eyes European Expansion, the Only Question is When," The Globe and Mail, November 12, 2018.
   https://www.theglobeandmail.com/sports/article-nhl-eyes-european-expansion-the-only-question-is-when/

GLOSSARY

amateur: a player who is not paid to participate in a sport

bye: advancing to a further round of competition without having to play in a current one

breakaway: a play in which no defender but the goalie stands between an offensive player with the puck and the goal

concussion: a bruise to the brain

controversy: a long, often heated, debate or disagreement

CTE: short for chronic traumatic encephalopathy, a degenerative brain disease caused by repeated head trauma

dynasty: a period of dominance by one team that lasts at least for several seasons

expansion team: a new team added to an existing league

face-off: a way to begin play by having a member from each team face each other and compete for the puck that is dropped between them

franchise: a team with membership in a professional sports league

power play: a period of action in which one team has more players on the ice than the opposing team due to a penalty on the opposing team

professional: a player who is paid to participate in a sport

seed: a team's rank in the playoffs

shutout: a game in which one team fails to score and loses

trustee: a person who has control or powers of administration

upset: a game or series in which the underdog wins

FURTHER READING

Books

Herman, Gail. *What Is the Stanley Cup?* New York: Penguin Workshop, 2019.

Kortemeier, Todd. *Total Hockey*. Minneapolis: SportsZone, an imprint of Abdo Publishing, 2017.

Websites

ESPN.com—NHL
http://www.espn.com/nhl/

Hockey Hall of Fame
https://www.hhof.com/

Hockey Reference
https://www.hockey-reference.com/

NHL.com
https://www.nhl.com/

NWHL.com
https://www.nwhl.zone/

INDEX

ABOUT THE AUTHOR

Matt Doeden began his career as a sportswriter. Since then he's spent more then a decade writing and editing more than 100 children's nonfiction books. His books *The Super Bowl: Chasing Football Immortality*, *The Negro Leagues: Celebrating Baseball's Unsung Heroes*, *The World Series: Baseball's Biggest Stage*, *Sandy Koufax*, and *Tom Brady: Unlikely Champion* were Junior Library Guid selections. Doeden lives in Minnesota with his wife and two chidren.

PHOTO ACKNOWLEDGMENTS

The images in this book are used with the permission of: © Bettmann/Getty Images, p. 4; © Jeff Bottari/National Hockey League/Getty Images, p.6; © Bruce Bennett Studios/Getty Images, pp. 9, 10, 12; © History and Art Collection/Alamy Stock Photo, p. 13; © marinat197/Shutterstock, p. 13 (side bar backgrounds) © Bruce Bennett Studios/Getty Images, p. 14; © Bettmann/Getty Images, p. 16; © Charles Bjorgen/Star Tribune/Getty Images, p. 17; Picturenow/Getty Images, p. 18; © Buyenlarge/Getty Images, p. 20; © Bruce Bennett Studios/Getty Images, pp . 21, 22, 23; © Bettmann/Getty Images, p. 25; © Graig Abel Collection/Getty Images Sport/Getty Images, p. 26; © Associated Press/Doug Pizac, p. 28; © Bruce Bennett Studios/Getty Images, pp. 29, 31, 32; © Associated Press, p. 33; © Bruce Bennett Studios/Getty Images, p. 34; © Nicholas T. LoVerde/Cal Sport Media/Alamy, p. 35; © Bruce Bennett Studios/Getty Images, p. 36; © Dave Sandford/National Hockey League/Getty Images, p. 38; © Brian Babineau/National Hockey League/Getty Images, p. 40; © Bruce Bennett Studios/Getty Images, pp. 41, 43 (two photos); © Bettmann/Getty Images, p. 44; © Bruce Bennett Studios/Getty Images, pp. 46, 47; © Denis Brodeur/National Hockey League/Getty Images, pp. 48, 49; © Bruce Bennett Studios/Getty Images, pp. 50, 51; © Associated Press/Donna McWilliam, p. 52; © Associated Press/Gene Puskar, p. 53; © Jeanine Leech/Icon Sportswire/Getty Images, p. 55; © Chris Seward/Raleigh News & Observer/Tribune News Service/Getty Images, p. 57; © Dave Sandford/National Hockey League/Getty Images, p. 58; © Xinhua/Lukasz Laskowski/Getty Images, p. 59.

Cover: © Rich Gagnon/Stringer/Getty Images Sport/Getty Images; Jacket flap: © Bruce Bennett Studios/Getty Images Sport/Getty Images; © Title page: klarka0608/Shutterstock.